EDWARD P. MARTIN

Catholic Healing and Deliverance Prayer Book

The Ultimate Catholic Prayer Book for Healing, Protection, and Freedom

Contents

Introduction

Welcome to this collection of prayers for healing and deliverance—a spiritual companion designed to guide you closer to the heart of God, who is the ultimate source of all restoration and peace. Whether you are seeking physical healing, emotional freedom, reconciliation in relationships, or deliverance from spiritual oppression, these prayers are offered as tools to help you surrender your burdens to the One who bore them all on the cross. Lo

As Catholics, we believe that God desires our wholeness— body, mind, and soul. Yet, we also know that life is filled with challenges, wounds, and struggles that can leave us feeling broken, weary, or distant from Him. In moments like these, prayer becomes more than words; it becomes an act of faith, a cry for mercy, and a step toward divine intervention. Through prayer, we open ourselves to God's transformative grace, trusting that He hears us and responds according to His perfect will.

While prayer is essential, it is most effective when accompanied by the sacraments, which are the primary means of encountering Christ's grace. Two sacraments, in particular, play a vital role in the journey toward healing: **Confession** and the **Eucharist** .

The **Sacrament of Confession** restores us to full communion with God by cleansing us of sin and removing the barriers that hinder His grace. If you carry unconfessed sins, I encourage you to seek this sacrament as a first step toward reconciliation. It is in Confession that we experience the mercy of Christ, who longs to heal and restore us.

The **Eucharist** , the "source and summit of the Christian life," nourishes us with the very presence of Jesus Christ. In receiving Him in the Blessed Sacrament, we are strengthened spiritually to face life's trials and are reminded that He walks with us in every moment of suffering and joy. Regular participation in the Eucharist sustains our faith and deepens our union with Christ, making our prayers even more fruitful.

Before praying the petitions in this book, take time to prepare your heart. Examine your conscience, seek forgiveness for your sins, and resolve to turn away from anything that separates you from God's love. Pair these prayers with frequent participation in Confession and the Eucharist, allowing these sacraments to magnify the graces you receive through prayer.

This book is not merely a compilation of prayers—it is an invitation to encounter Jesus Christ, the Divine Physician, who longs to heal every area of your life. Each section addresses a specific need, offering prayers rooted in Scripture, tradition, and the timeless wisdom of the Church. These prayers are meant to be prayed with sincerity, humility, and confidence in God's power to work miracles—even when the answers come in ways we least expect.

Remember, dear reader, that while these prayers are powerful, their efficacy depends entirely on your union with Christ and your willingness to cooperate with His grace. Be patient, persistent, and open to the ways God may choose to answer your petitions. Sometimes healing comes instantly; other times, it unfolds gradually, shaping us into vessels of greater holiness and trust.

Let this book serve as a beacon of light during dark seasons, a source of comfort in times of trial, and a reminder that no wound is too deep, no burden too heavy, and no sin too great for God's boundless mercy. As you pray, let your heart echo the words of the Psalmist:

"The Lord is near to the brokenhearted and saves the crushed in spirit" (Psalm 34:18).

Come, then, and enter into this sacred dialogue with the Father, Son, and Holy Spirit. Bring your pain, your hopes, and your dreams to the foot of the cross, confident that you are loved beyond measure and that nothing is impossible for God.

May God bless you abundantly as you seek His healing touch. Amen.

I

Preparation

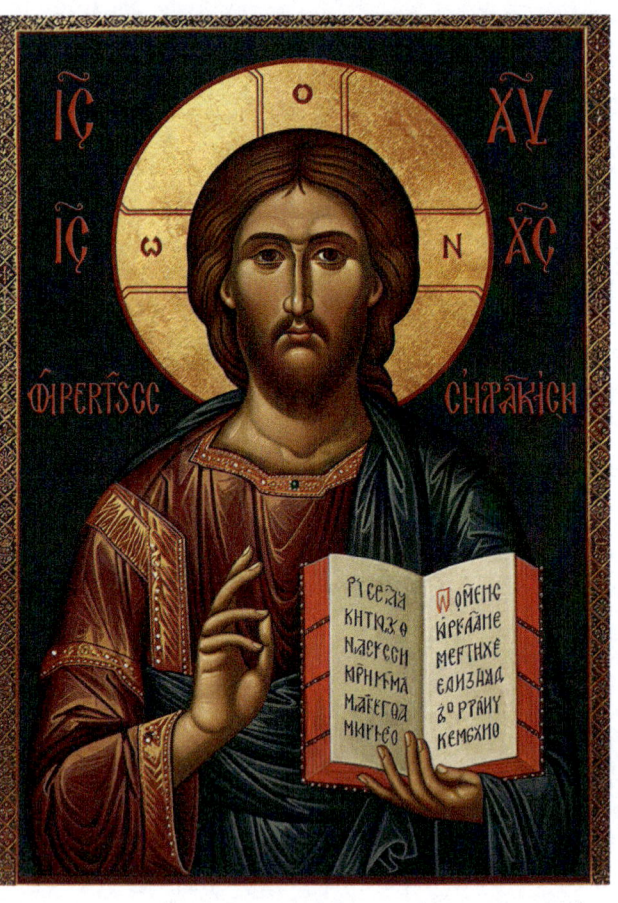

The Path to Healing Begins with Reconciliation

Healing—whether physical, emotional, or spiritual—is a gift from God, but it does not come automatically. It flows from a heart that is open to His grace and aligned with His will. In the Gospel of John, Jesus reminds us: *"I am the vine; you are the branches. Whoever remains in me and I in him will bear much fruit, because without me you can do nothing"* (John 15:5). True healing begins with reconciliation—restoring our relationship with God and others.

The prayers in this book are not magical formulas or words spoken into the void. Their efficacy depends entirely on the state of our hearts and our union with Christ. If we harbor sin, resentment, or unforgiveness, these obstacles block the flow of divine grace. Therefore, before diving into the prayers, let us first prepare ourselves by seeking reconciliation with God and neighbor

Why Reconciliation Matters

Reconciliation is at the heart of the Christian life. When we sin, we damage our relationship with God and often hurt those around us. Sin creates barriers that hinder our ability to receive His healing touch. As Jesus teaches in the Sermon on the Mount:

> "If you bring your gift to the altar and there recall that your brother has anything against you, leave your gift at the altar, go first and be reconciled with your brother, and then come and offer your gift" (*Matthew 5:23-24*).

God desires mercy above sacrifice. He longs for us to approach Him with clean hands and pure hearts. Through the Sacrament of Confession, we experience the joy of being forgiven and restored to full communion with Him. This sacrament cleanses us of sin, renews our souls, and opens the door to divine healing.

But reconciliation is not only about restoring our relationship with God—it also involves mending broken relationships with others. Unresolved conflicts, anger, or bitterness can weigh heavily on our hearts, preventing us from fully receiving God's peace. By humbling ourselves, asking forgiveness, and extending mercy to others, we create space for God's transformative love to work within us.

Examination of Conscience

To begin the journey of reconciliation, we must first examine our consciences. This process helps us identify areas where we have fallen short in loving God and others. Take some time to reflect on the following questions:

First Commandment: "I am the Lord your God; you shall have no other gods before me."

1. Have I placed anything—work, money, entertainment, relationships—ahead of my love for God?
2. Have I neglected prayer, Mass, or the sacraments due to busyness or indifference?
3. Have I engaged in superstitious practices (e.g., astrology, tarot cards) or shown interest in occult activities?

Second Commandment: "You shall not take the name of the Lord your God in vain."

1. Have I used God's name carelessly, irreverently, or in anger?
2. Have I cursed, sworn falsely, or blasphemed?

Third Commandment: "Remember to keep holy the Sabbath day."

1. Have I missed Mass on Sundays or holy days of obligation without a valid reason?
2. Have I treated Sundays as a day of rest and worship, or have I allowed worldly concerns to dominate?

Fourth Commandment: "Honor your father and mother."

1. Have I shown respect, gratitude, and obedience to my parents (if applicable)?

2. As a parent, have I provided for my children spiritually, emotionally, and materially?
3. Have I honored authority figures in society, such as teachers, employers, or government leaders?

Fifth Commandment: "You shall not kill."

1. Have I harbored anger, hatred, or resentment toward anyone?
2. Have I physically harmed or wished harm upon another person?
3. Have I supported or condoned practices that violate the sanctity of life, such as abortion or euthanasia?

Sixth and Ninth Commandments: "You shall not commit adultery" / "You shall not covet your neighbor's spouse."

1. Have I engaged in impure thoughts, words, or actions?
2. Have I been unfaithful to my spouse or violated the dignity of marriage?
3. Have I consumed pornography or objectified others?

Seventh and Tenth Commandments: "You shall not steal" / "You shall not covet your neighbor's goods."

1. Have I stolen, cheated, or failed to repay debts?
2. Have I been greedy or envious of others' possessions?
3. Have I given generously to those in need, or have I been stingy with my time, talent, and treasure?

Eighth Commandment: "You shall not bear false witness

against your neighbor."

1. Have I lied, gossiped, slandered, or spread rumors about others?
2. Have I judged others harshly or assumed the worst about their intentions?
3. Have I spoken poorly of the Church or its teachings?

Be honest with yourself and with God. Remember, He already knows your heart. The purpose of this examination is not to discourage you but to help you recognize areas where you need His mercy and grace.

Act of Contrition

Once you have examined your conscience, express sorrow for your sins through the *Act of Contrition* . This prayer acknowledges your offenses against God and resolves to amend your life. Pray it slowly and sincerely, allowing its words to penetrate your heart:

> *O my God, I am heartily sorry for having offended You,*
> *And I detest all my sins because I dread the loss of*
> *heaven and the pains of hell;*
> *But most of all because they offend You, my God,*
> *Who are all good and deserving of all my love.*
> *I firmly resolve, with the help of Your grace,*
> *To confess my sins, to do penance, and to amend my life.*
> *Amen.*

Let this act of contrition be more than just words. Offer it with genuine remorse and a desire to change. God's mercy is infinite, and He eagerly awaits your return.

The Power of Forgiveness

Forgiveness is one of the most profound acts of love and humility we can offer. Jesus taught us to pray, *"Forgive us our trespasses, as we forgive those who trespass against us"* (Matthew 6:12). Unforgiveness creates barriers—not only between us and others but also between us and God. It can weigh heavily on our hearts, causing emotional and even physical suffering.

To prepare your heart for healing and reconciliation, consider praying the following forgiveness prayer written by Father Robert DeGrandis, SSJ. This prayer invites you to release bitterness, seek peace, and open yourself to God's transformative love. It covers many areas of life where forgiveness may be needed, including family, friends, co-workers, and even enemies. Let the Holy Spirit guide you as you pray, bringing to mind any additional people or situations that need forgiveness.

The Forgiveness Prayer

Lord Jesus Christ, I ask today to forgive everyone in my life. I know that You will give me strength to forgive and I thank You that You love me more than I love myself and want my happiness more than I desire it for myself.

Lord Jesus, I want to be free from the feelings of resentment, bitterness, and unforgiveness toward You for the times I thought You sent death, hardships, financial difficulties, punishments, and sickness in our family.

Lord, I forgive myself for my sins, faults, and failings.

For all that is truly bad in myself or all that I think is bad, I do forgive myself. For indulging in the occult, Ouija boards, horoscopes, séances, fortune-telling, lucky charms, [dream catchers]; for taking my name in vain; for not worshiping You; for hurting my parents; for getting drunk; [for the use of illegal drugs]; [for the misuse of legal drugs]; for sins against my purity; for adultery; for abortion; for stealing; for lying—I am truly forgiving myself today. Thank You, Lord, for Your grace at this moment.

I truly forgive my mother. I forgive her for all the times she hurt me, resented me, was angry with me, and for all the times she punished me [unjustly]. I forgive her for the times she preferred my brothers and sisters to me. I forgive her for the times she told me I was dumb, ugly, stupid, the worst of the children, or that I cost the family a lot of money. For the times she told me I was unwanted, an accident, a mistake, or not what she expected. [For any negativity, gossip, manipulation, or bad example], I forgive her.

I forgive my father. I forgive him for any lack of support, any lack of love, affection, or attention. I forgive him for any lack of time, for not giving me his companionship, for his drinking or arguing and fighting with my mother or other children. For his severe punishments, for desertion, for being away from home, for divorcing my mother, or for any running around, I do forgive him.

The forgiveness for mother and father can be interchangeable depending on your story.

Lord, I extend forgiveness to my sisters and brothers. I

forgive those who rejected me, lied about me, hated me, resented me, competed for my parents' love, those who hurt me, who physically harmed me. For those who were too severe on me, punished me, or made my life unpleasant in any way, I do forgive them.

Lord, I forgive my spouse for lack of love, affection, consideration, support, attention, communication, for faults, failings, weaknesses, and those other acts or words that hurt or disturb me.

Jesus, I forgive my children for their lack of respect, obedience, love, attention, support, warmth, understanding; their bad habits, falling away from the Church, and bad actions which disturb me.

My God, I forgive my in-laws—mother, father, son or daughter-in-law, sister and brother-in-law, and other relatives by marriage. For their lack of love, words of criticism, thoughts, actions, or omissions which injure and cause pain, I do forgive them.

Please help me to forgive my relatives, my grandmother and grandfather who may have interfered in our family, been possessive of my parents, who may have caused confusion or turned one parent against the other.

Jesus, help me to forgive my co-workers who are disagreeable or make life miserable for me. For those who push their work off on me, gossip about me, won't cooperate with me, try to take my job, I do forgive them.

My neighbors need to be forgiven, Lord. For all their noise, letting their property run down, [not training their pets properly], not taking in their trash cans, being prejudiced and running down the neighborhood, I do forgive them.

I now forgive my clergyman, [ministers], my congregation, and my church for all their lack of support, pettiness, bad sermons, lack of friendliness, not affirming me as they should, not providing me with inspiration, for not using me in a key position, for not inviting me to serve in a major capacity, and for any other hurt they have inflicted—I do forgive them today.

Lord, I forgive all professional people who have hurt me in any way—doctors, nurses, police officers, hospital workers, lawyers, contractors. For anything they did to me unjustly, I truly forgive them.

Lord, I forgive my employer for not paying me enough money, for not appreciating my work, for being unkind and unreasonable with me, for being angry and unfriendly, for not promoting me, and for not complimenting me on my work.

Lord, I forgive my schoolteachers, professors, and instructors of the past, as well as the present. For those who punished me, humiliated me, insulted me, treated me unjustly, made fun of me, called me dumb or stupid, made me stay after school.

Lord, I forgive my friends who have let me down, lost contact with me, do not support me, were not available when I needed help, borrowed money and did not return it, gossiped about me.

Lord Jesus, I especially pray for the grace of forgiveness for that one person in life who has hurt me the most. I ask to forgive anyone who I consider my greatest enemy, the one who I said I would never forgive.

Thank You, Jesus, that I am free of the evil of unforgiveness. Let Your Holy Spirit fill me with light and let

every dark area of my mind be enlightened.
  AMEN.

Promise to Go to Confession

For those who have committed serious sins, the next step is to seek the Sacrament of Penance. If you have unconfessed mortal sins, make a firm commitment to go to confession as soon as possible. For venial sins, regular confession strengthens your soul and deepens your relationship with God.

Here are some practical tips for preparing for confession:

1. Write down your sins if it helps you organize your thoughts.
2. Pray beforehand, asking the Holy Spirit to guide you.
3. Trust in the priest's role as a minister of Christ's mercy—he is there to help, not judge.

Even if you feel unworthy or ashamed, remember that God rejoices when we repent. As the prophet Isaiah declares:

"Though your sins are like scarlet, they shall be as white as snow; though they are red as crimson, they shall be like wool" *(Isaiah 1:18).*

The Role of Prayer in Healing

With a reconciled heart, you are now ready to approach the prayers in this book. These prayers are tools for deepening your trust in God and persevering through trials. They are not magic spells but expressions of faith, hope, and surrender to

His will.

Prayer works hand-in-hand with reconciliation. It invites God into every aspect of your life, opening doors for His grace to heal what is broken. Be patient and persistent—God hears your prayers, even if His answers come in ways you don't expect.

As St. Augustine once said:

"Our hearts are restless until they rest in You, O Lord."

May your journey through this book lead you closer to the One who heals, restores, and redeems.

Closing Reflection

Reconciliation is the first step toward experiencing God's abundant mercy. By humbling ourselves, examining our consciences, and seeking forgiveness, we clear the path for His grace to flow freely. Let us move forward with confidence, knowing that God delights in welcoming us home. As King David prayed:

"Create in me a clean heart, O God, and renew a
steadfast spirit within me"
(Psalm 51:10).

II

Prayers for Generational Healing

2

Breaking Generational Curses

"The Spirit of the Lord God is upon me... to proclaim liberty to captives and freedom to prisoners."
— Isaiah 61:1

Heavenly Father,

Eternal and merciful God, source of all life and holiness, I humbly come before Your divine presence in the name of Your beloved Son, Our Lord Jesus Christ. With faith in His saving grace and the power of His precious Blood, I present myself before You to renounce every generational curse that has ever cast a shadow upon my family line.

Through the Cross of Christ, death has been conquered and sin rendered powerless. I proclaim that no curse, no inherited wound, no sinful pattern passed down through generations holds dominion over me or those who belong to the household of God. In the light of the Gospel, I reject every influence of evil that has taken root in my ancestry—be it idolatry, occult practices, hatred, violence, adultery, or any other offense against Your holy law.

By the power of the Holy Spirit and the intercession of Jesus, the one Mediator between God and man, I break every chain of sin that has bound my forebears. I call upon the sacred Name of Jesus, before whom every knee must bow, to loose the bonds of iniquity and heal the wounds of generations past.

I repent not only for my own sins but also for those committed by my ancestors, asking for the grace of purification and renewal. Heal our family tree, O Lord, grafting it into the true vine, Your Son Jesus Christ, that we may bear fruits worthy of repentance and walk in newness of life.

Pour forth upon me the gifts of the Holy Spirit—wisdom, understanding, counsel, fortitude, knowledge, piety, and fear of the Lord—that I may live as a faithful witness of Your love and truth. May my life become a blessing to those who come after me, leaving behind a legacy of faith, virtue, and devotion to You.

And finally, I entrust my entire lineage to the Immaculate Heart of Mary, Mother of God and Mother of the Church. Just as she stood beneath the Cross, interceding with faith and love, so too may she cover my family with her maternal protection and lead us to her Divine Son. Through her powerful intercession, may purity replace corruption, peace replace discord, and holiness replace sin in every generation to come.

We ask this through Christ our Lord, and by the merits of His most holy Mother, Mary ever Virgin.

Amen.

3

Healing Genetic Weaknesses

"He himself bore our sins in his body on the cross, so that we might die to sin and live to righteousness. By His wounds you have been healed."

— 1 Peter 2:24

Lord Jesus Christ,

Divine Physician of souls and bodies, I humbly lift up to You the burdens carried in my very flesh—those genetic weaknesses, predispositions, and vulnerabilities passed down through my family line. Whether they manifest as physical ailments, mental health struggles, emotional wounds, or spiritual fragility, I bring them all before Your merciful throne.

You are the Lord who fashioned the human body in wisdom and love, and though sin and suffering have marred its perfection, You remain its healer and restorer. I renounce every effect of original sin and personal sin that has weakened my lineage, and I ask for Your healing touch upon every cell, organ, and system within me. Heal also the memories stored in my body, the traumas inherited from generations past, and the sorrows that linger in my blood.

By Your holy Cross and precious Blood, by Your sacred Passion and Resurrection, I claim the promise of Scripture: "By His wounds we are healed." I place my trust in Your power to restore what has been broken, to renew what has grown weak, and to breathe new life into what has known only pain.

O Lord, where there has been weakness, send forth Your strength; where there has been illness, grant vitality; where there has been despair, pour out hope; where there has been fear, instill peace. Make all things new in Your Sacred Heart, and let Your grace perfect what nature lacks.

I unite my sufferings to Yours, dear Jesus, offering them with You, through You, and in You for the glory of the Father and the salvation of souls. May my body become a temple of the Holy Spirit and my life a testimony to Your mercy.

And now, I entrust myself and my entire family line to the tender care of Mary, Mother of Mercy and Health of the Sick. As she once cradled You, the Divine Healer, in her arms, may she wrap her mantle of protection around me and all who share my blood. Through her Immaculate Heart, may healing flow through my lineage, restoring body, mind, and soul unto eternal life.

We ask this through Christ our Lord, and by the prayers of His most holy Mother, Mary ever Virgin.

4

Renouncing Family Patterns of Sin

"For the wages of sin is death, but the free gift of God is eternal life in Christ Jesus our Lord."
— ***Romans 6:23***

Heavenly Father,

God of mercy and redemption, I come before You in humility and repentance, acknowledging the sins that have wounded my family across generations. Today, by the grace of Your Son and the power of the Holy Spirit, I renounce every sinful pattern that has taken root in my lineage—addiction and abuse, infidelity and division, bitterness and pride, selfishness and neglect, and any other vice that has brought pain, brokenness, and separation from You.

I repent not only for my own sins, but also for those committed by my ancestors, whose choices have left echoes in my life and the lives of those I love. I reject the lies of the enemy that say these cycles must continue, that I am bound to repeat what others have done before me. In the name of Jesus Christ, I break every chain of sin that seeks to hold sway over my heart and home.

O Lord, You are faithful and rich in mercy. I open my soul to Your transforming grace, which alone can heal what is broken and restore what has been lost. Help me to walk in the light of Your truth, to live as a child of God and a temple of the Holy Spirit. Make me an instrument of Your peace, a beacon of holiness in my family line, and a witness to Your saving power.

Grant me the strength to forgive, the courage to change, and the wisdom to raise up a new generation rooted in love, virtue, and faith. Let Your Kingdom come into my household, and let Your will be done in all things.

And now, I place myself and my entire family under the protection of the Blessed Virgin Mary, Mother of God and Queen of Families. Just as she nurtured the Holy Family with purity and devotion, so too may her maternal care purify our hearts, guide our steps, and lead us all to her Divine Son. May her Immaculate Heart triumph in our home, and may sin no longer have dominion over us.

We ask this through Christ our Lord, who lives and reigns with You in the unity of the Holy Spirit, one God forever and ever,

and by the prayers of His most holy Mother, Mary ever Virgin.

Amen.

5

Consecration of Family Line to Jesus

"You are My beloved Son; with You I am well pleased."
— Mark 1:11

Lord Jesus Christ,

Eternal Word of the Father, King of all creation, and Savior of every soul who has ever lived, I humbly come before You today to offer a sacred act of love and surrender. With all the faith my heart can muster, I consecrate to You my entire family line—from the earliest of my ancestors to the generations yet unborn. I present to Your Most Sacred Heart every branch of my family tree, both living and deceased, known and unknown, that they may be sanctified by Your grace and united in Your divine love.

O Sacred Heart of Jesus, burning with love for all humanity, become the center and foundation of my family. Be our refuge in times of trial, our strength in moments of weakness, and our light when darkness seeks to enter our hearts and homes. May Your holy Name be honored in every word spoken among us, and may Your commandment of love shape every relationship within our lineage.

I renounce every work of the evil one that has sought to divide, wound, or enslave my family through sin, brokenness, or spiritual blindness. Break every stronghold of darkness that has taken root in our history, and replace it with the fire of Your Holy Spirit. Heal what is wounded, restore what is lost, and transform what remains into a living testimony of Your mercy and redemption.

I entrust my family entirely into Your most tender care, knowing that You desire only our good and long to lead us to eternal life. May Your will be done in each of our lives, now and forever. Let us live not for ourselves alone, but for the glory of God and the building up of Your Kingdom on earth.

And finally, I place my entire family under the protection of the Blessed Virgin Mary, Mother of God and Queen of Families, and beneath the patronage of St. Joseph, Guardian of the Holy Family. As they nurtured and safeguarded the Child Jesus, so too may they watch over us with heavenly care. Through the intercession of Mary, Seat of Wisdom and Refuge of Sinners, may purity, peace, and holiness dwell in our hearts and homes from generation to generation.

We ask this through You, Lord Jesus, our Savior and Redeemer, and by the prayers of Your most holy Mother, Mary ever Virgin, and of all the saints who rejoice in Your eternal kingdom.

Amen.

6

Intercession for Ancestors Who Have Passed Away

"I am the resurrection and the life; whoever believes in Me, though he die, yet shall he live."
— ***John 11:25***

Eternal Father,

God of infinite mercy and everlasting compassion, I humbly lift up before Your holy throne the souls of my ancestors who have gone before me into the next life. With faith in Your boundless love and hope in the promises of Your Son, I commend them once again to Your divine care.

For those who may not have fully known You in this life, or who lived far from the warmth of Your grace, I implore the redemptive power of Christ's Passion, Death, and Resurrection. By the merits of His Most Sacred Heart, forgive their sins, cleanse their souls, and welcome them into the joy of eternal light. May purgatory hold no lasting claim upon them, and may they now rejoice in the fullness of Your presence.

If they already dwell in heaven, O Lord, I ask that You strengthen their intercession on behalf of our family. Let their prayers rise like incense before Your throne, and may their holy witness—known or unknown—inspire us to greater faithfulness and holiness. Through their heavenly advocacy, help us to break every chain that binds us to sin and lead us ever closer to Your sacred Heart.

Grant us, Your children still on earth, the grace to honor them by living lives worthy of our calling in Christ. May we continue their legacy where it was good, and where it fell short, may we repair it through repentance, charity, and fidelity to the Gospel.

We thank You for the communion of saints—the wondrous union of heaven and earth—where death does not sever our bonds but transforms them in love. In Christ, we are one across time and eternity, united by hope, sealed in charity, and destined for glory.

And finally, I entrust all my ancestors and the entire lineage of my family to the Immaculate Heart of Mary, Mother of Mercy and Refuge of Sinners. As she stood at the foot of the Cross and shared in the redemptive suffering of her Divine Son, may she now welcome our beloved dead into paradise and guide us, her children on earth, safely home.

We ask this through Christ our Lord, the Resurrection and the Life,

and by the prayers of His most holy Mother, Mary ever
Virgin,

Queen of All Saints.

Amen.

7

Invoking the Holy Spirit for Transformation

"And when the day of Pentecost had come, they were all together in one place. And suddenly there came from heaven a sound like a mighty rushing wind... and they were all filled with the Holy Spirit."

— Acts 2:1–4

Come, Holy Spirit,

Paraclete and Giver of Life, eternal Love proceeding from the Father and the Son, descend upon my family line as fire from heaven. Purify us from every stain of sin, cleanse our hearts from impurity, and renew the spirit within us. Let Your divine flame burn away all that is contrary to God—discord, selfishness, bitterness, and despair—and fill us with the fragrance of holiness.

O Divine Sanctifier, heal what is wounded, restore what has

been stolen by the enemy, and transform our weaknesses into strengths through grace. Where there is sorrow, pour forth Your joy; where there is failure, raise up testimonies of redemption; where there is division, plant unity and peace. Make our family a dwelling place of Your presence, a temple of Your glory.

Pour out upon us the fullness of Your gifts: wisdom to discern truth, understanding to know the ways of God, counsel to walk in righteousness, fortitude to endure trials, knowledge to grow in faith, piety to honor You in word and deed, and fear of the Lord that leads to true repentance and reverence.

Let the fruits of Your holy presence abound in our lives—love that imitates Christ, joy that remains steadfast in trial, peace that surpasses understanding, patience that endures, kindness that heals, goodness that builds up, faithfulness that stands firm, gentleness that calms, and self-control that reflects Your mastery over our hearts.

Teach us to live not according to the flesh, but as children of God, reflecting the image of Christ in thought, word, and action. May our lives be a living witness to Your transforming power, drawing others to the light of the Gospel.

And now, I entrust my entire family to the Immaculate Heart of Mary, Mother of the Church and Mediatrix of All Graces. As she prayed with the Apostles at Pentecost, may she intercede for us, that we may receive the fullness of the Holy Spirit and become faithful disciples of her Son. May her maternal care guard our hearts, guide our steps, and lead us all to Jesus, the

Way, the Truth, and the Life.

We ask this through Christ our Lord, who lives and reigns with the Father in the unity of the Holy Spirit,

and by the prayers of His most holy Mother, Mary ever Virgin,

Queen of the Apostles and Mother of Divine Love.

Amen.

8

Thanksgiving for Deliverance and Restoration

"Give thanks to the Lord, for He is good; His mercy endures forever."
— Psalm 107:1

O Gracious and Eternal Lord,

King of Heaven and Earth, Fountain of Mercy and Source of all blessings, I come before You with a heart overflowing in gratitude. I thank You for hearing my prayers and answering them according to Your holy will. In Your infinite love, You have broken the chains of generational sin and healed the wounds of the past that once held sway over my family line.

I rejoice in the freedom won for us by Your beloved Son, Our Lord Jesus Christ, who has redeemed us from bondage and restored our dignity as children of God. Thank You for redeeming what was lost, for healing what was broken, and for filling us with the life-giving power of the Holy Spirit.

May Your blessings flow like rivers through our family, bringing new life, renewed hope, and the light of salvation to all who follow after us. Let the fruit of Your grace be evident in every generation—holiness of life, unity of purpose, and steadfast faith in Your promises.

Grant me and all my loved ones the strength to remain faithful in times of trial, the wisdom to walk in Your commandments, and the courage to bear witness to Your truth in word and deed. May we never forget the wonders You have done for us, nor grow weary in doing good, knowing that in due time, we will reap if we do not lose heart.

And now, I lift up my voice in praise and thanksgiving, joining the angels and saints in eternal worship. To You alone, O Lord, be all honor, glory, and blessing forever and ever.

Finally, I entrust all the blessings you have poured out upon my family into the Immaculate Heart of Mary, Mother of Divine Providence and Queen of the Family. As she faithfully pondered all things in her heart and followed Your divine plan, may she guide us always toward her Son, Jesus, the Way, the Truth, and the Life.

We bless and glorify You through Him, Christ our Lord,
    and by the prayers of His most holy Mother, Mary ever Virgin,
    and of all the saints who rejoice in Your eternal kingdom.
    Amen.

III

Prayers for Emotional Healing

9

Healing from Anxiety and Fear

*"Do not be afraid, for I am with you; do not be dismayed,
for I am your God. I will strengthen you and help you."*

— Isaiah 41:10

Lord Jesus Christ,

Divine Physician of souls and bodies, I come before You with
a heart weighed down by anxiety and fear. The storms of
uncertainty rage within me, and the shadows of worry cloud
my mind. Yet I know, O Lord, that You are my refuge and my
strength—my ever-present help in times of trouble.

In the midst of my distress, remind me of Your sacred promise:
"Come to Me, all you who labor and are burdened, and I will
give you rest." (Matthew 11:28) Teach me, dear Savior, to cast
all my cares upon You, for I know that You care deeply for me.

By the power of Your Most Sacred Heart, quiet the tempests within my soul and replace my fears with Your perfect peace— one that surpasses all understanding and guards my heart and mind in Christ Jesus.

Strengthen my trust in Your divine providence, even when the path ahead seems unclear. Help me to surrender my worries into Your wounded hands, believing that You hold all things in love. Let my heart echo the words of St. Peter: "Cast all your anxieties on Him, because He cares for you." (1 Peter 5:7)

Fill me anew with the fire of Your Holy Spirit, the Consoler and Light of the world, who reminds me that I am never alone. You are always with me—even when I cannot feel Your presence. Quiet every voice of despair, silence the lies of the enemy, and renew in me a spirit of confidence, courage, and hope.

I renounce all fear in the name of Jesus, and I declare with faith: The Lord is my Shepherd; I shall not want. May Your grace transform my heart, making it a dwelling place of peace, joy, and trust.

And finally, I entrust my anxious heart to the Immaculate Heart of Mary, Mother of Mercy and Refuge of Sinners. As she pondered all things in her heart and trusted in God's plan, may she wrap me in her maternal protection and lead me closer to her Son, the Prince of Peace. Through her powerful intercession, may fear be replaced by faith, turmoil by tranquility, and sorrow by divine consolation.

We ask this through Christ our Lord,

and by the prayers of His most holy Mother, Mary ever Virgin,

Queen of Peace and Advocate of All Who Suffer.

Amen.

10

Comfort in Grief and Loss

"Blessed are those who mourn, for they shall be comforted."
— ***Matthew 5:4***

Heavenly Father,

God of infinite mercy and Eternal Consoler, I come before You with a heart weighed down by sorrow. The pain of loss pierces my soul, and grief holds me in its tender yet painful embrace. In my anguish, I lift my eyes to You, knowing that You are close to the brokenhearted and that You draw near to those crushed in spirit.

You, O Lord, are the Resurrection and the Life. I bring my beloved dead into the light of Your love, trusting in Your boundless compassion. If they walked faithfully in Your ways, grant them the crown of eternal joy in Your heavenly kingdom.

If they faltered or wandered far, I beg You—pour forth the merits of Your Son's sacrifice and open the gates of mercy wide, that they may find peace in Your embrace.

O Lord, You are the balm of our suffering and the hope of our hearts. Heal the emptiness left behind and fill it with the warmth of Your holy presence. Teach me to grieve with hope, rooted in the promise of resurrection, and sustained by the knowledge that death does not sever what love has united. One day, by Your grace, we shall be reunited in the fullness of Your Kingdom, where there will be no more tears, no more sorrow, only life without end.

I thank You for being my refuge and strength in this time of mourning. Be my light amid shadows, my peace amid turmoil, and my hope when all else fades.

And finally, I entrust my sorrow into the arms of the Blessed Virgin Mary, Mother of Sorrows and Queen of Heaven. As she stood beneath the Cross, bearing the weight of unspeakable grief with faith and love, may she now wrap me in her maternal comfort and lead me closer to her Divine Son. Through her Immaculate Heart, may healing flow into my wounded heart, and may the promise of eternal life shine ever brighter in my soul.

We ask this through Christ our Lord, the Resurrection and the Life,
    and by the prayers of His most holy Mother, Mary ever Virgin,
    Consoler of the Afflicted and Hope of Christians.

11

Release from Bitterness and Resentment

"Be kind to one another, tenderhearted, forgiving one another,
as God in Christ forgave you."
— Ephesians 4:32

Merciful Lord Jesus Christ,

Divine Healer of wounded hearts and Fountain of all mercy, I humbly come before You burdened by the weight of bitterness and resentment. I confess that these emotions have taken root within me, poisoning my soul and keeping me from experiencing the fullness of Your peace and joy.

I repent of allowing anger to dwell in my heart, of clinging to wounds long after they were inflicted, and of failing to extend to others the same forgiveness You so freely offer to me. Forgive me, O Lord, for holding on to what only brings death, and help me to surrender every hurt into Your wounded hands.

Today, by the power of Your Cross and the grace of the Holy Spirit, I choose to let go. I renounce every spirit of unforgiveness and break its hold over my heart. With the strength You alone provide, I forgive those who have wronged me—those who have wounded me through word or deed, knowingly or unknowingly. I ask that You soften my heart toward them, that I may see them not as enemies, but as souls loved by You, in need of mercy just as I am.

O Lord, uproot every bitter root from my soul and plant in its place the fruits of Your Holy Spirit—love, joy, peace, patience, kindness, goodness, faithfulness, gentleness, and self-control. Heal the memories that sting, restore the joy that was stolen, and teach me to walk in freedom, no longer enslaved by the past.

Transform my heart, dear Jesus, that it may reflect Your own Sacred Heart—overflowing with compassion, mercy, and love. Let me become an instrument of reconciliation in my home, my community, and the world, bearing witness to the healing power of the Gospel.

And finally, I entrust my wounded heart to the Immaculate Heart of Mary, Mother of Forgiveness and Refuge of Sinners. As she forgave from the foot of the Cross, may she intercede for me and teach me to love as You love—freely, fully, and forever. May her maternal care guard my soul and lead me always back to You, the source of all mercy.

We ask this through Christ our Lord, the Lamb of God who takes away the sins of the world,

and by the prayers of His most holy Mother, Mary ever Virgin,

Queen of Mercy and Advocate of All Who Suffer.

Amen.

12

Restoration of Self-Worth

"You formed my inmost being; You knit me together in my mother's womb. I praise You, for I am fearfully and wonderfully made."
— Psalm 139:13–14

Loving Father,

God of infinite dignity and boundless love, I come before You with a heart that longs to know its true worth. In moments of weakness and doubt, the voices of rejection, failure, and criticism rise within me, clouding my mind with lies and causing me to forget who I truly am in Your eyes.

Yet today, I return to the sacred truth: I am fearfully and wonderfully made in Your image and likeness. You formed me in secret, knitting me together in my mother's womb, and called me into existence not by accident, but by design. Every breath I take is a gift from You, and every beat of my heart echoes with the love You have poured out upon me since the moment of my conception.

O Lord, speak to the depths of my soul and awaken me to the reality of Your unconditional love. Remind me—deeply and personally—that I am chosen, forgiven, and called to holiness in Christ Jesus. Let Your Word be louder than every voice of condemnation, and let Your truth silence the enemy who seeks to rob me of joy, peace, and purpose.

Where there is shame, plant humility; where there is doubt, instill confidence rooted in grace; where there is insecurity, fill me with the knowledge that I am Your beloved child, redeemed by the Blood of Christ and sealed with the Holy Spirit. Nothing—nothing in heaven or on earth—can separate me from Your love.

I ask You, O Lord, to restore my sense of identity and dignity as a member of Your holy family. Heal the wounds of past failures and brokenness, and help me to walk boldly in the freedom of the children of God. May I see myself through Your eyes—not defined by sin or weakness, but transformed by grace and destined for eternal glory.

And finally, I entrust my wounded self-image and longing for acceptance into the Immaculate Heart of Mary, Mother of Mercy and Mirror of Justice. As she lived in perfect humility and purity, may she teach me to see myself as You see me—beautiful, beloved, and blessed. Under her maternal gaze, may my heart find healing, and may my life become a reflection of the holiness You desire for all Your children.

We ask this through Christ our Lord, who calls us to live in the fullness of His grace,

and by the prayers of His most holy Mother, Mary ever Virgin,

Queen of Heaven and Model of All Disciples.

13

Healing from Trauma and Abuse

"The Lord is near to the brokenhearted and rescues those who are crushed in spirit."
— Psalm 34:18

Compassionate Savior,

Divine Physician of wounded souls and Refuge of all who suffer, I come before You with a heart burdened by pain. Today, I lay at Your feet the deep wounds inflicted upon me through trauma and abuse—wounds that may not always be seen, but which run deep into the soul. Whether physical, emotional, or spiritual, these violations have left scars that only You can heal.

O Lord, You who were scourged, mocked, and betrayed know the depths of human suffering. I bring to You every moment of violation, every act of cruelty, every word that shattered my spirit. By the power of Your Cross and Resurrection, I ask that You pour forth Your healing balm upon every wound. Where there was harm, bring restoration; where there was shame, bestow dignity; where there was fear, plant peace.

Lord Jesus, You are the God of new beginnings. Where there was betrayal, heal my heart so that I may once again learn to trust. Where there was violation, cleanse me with the purity of Your grace. Where there was silence, give me voice; where there was confusion, grant clarity. Surround me with Your protective embrace, shield me from further harm, and raise up holy boundaries around my life.

Give me the courage to face my past without being enslaved by it, knowing that You walk beside me each step of the way. Transform what was meant for evil into a testimony of Your mercy. Turn the ashes of my suffering into a crown of beauty, and my pain into purpose for Your glory.

I unite my wounds to Yours, dear Jesus, offering them with You, through You, and in You for the salvation of souls and the triumph of love. Heal not only what is broken within me, but also renew my relationships, restore my sense of safety, and help me to live freely as a child of God.

And finally, I entrust my entire journey of healing into the Immaculate Heart of Mary, Mother of All Mercy and Refuge of Sinners. As she stood beneath the Cross, sharing in Your sorrow with faith and love, may she now wrap me in her maternal care. May she lead me ever closer to her Divine Son, the true Healer of our hearts, and teach me how to live in the light of His redeeming love.

We ask this through Christ our Lord, the Suffering Servant

who brings healing to the world,
and by the prayers of His most holy Mother, Mary ever Virgin,
Queen of Peace and Comforter of the Afflicted.
Amen

14

Freedom from Depression and Despair

"The light shines in the darkness, and the darkness has not overcome it."
—John 1:5

Faithful God,

Lord of mercy and Light of the world, I come before You shrouded in the heaviness of depression. A cloud of sorrow has settled over my mind and heart, draining joy from life and dimming the brightness of Your truth. Yet even now, in the midst of this inner night, I cling to the promise that Your light shines in the darkest places—and the darkness cannot overcome it.

O Jesus, Divine Physician of soul and body, draw near to me in this moment of deep despair. Speak peace to the storm within me, as You once calmed the winds and waves with a word. Remind me gently but powerfully that I am not forgotten—that You have created me for a purpose and that my life holds infinite meaning in Your loving hands.

Where there is numbness, awaken my heart; where there is emptiness, fill me with Your presence; where there is silence, let Your voice speak words of life. Strengthen me when I feel weak beyond weakness, and give me even the smallest spark of hope, knowing that with You, all things are possible.

Pour out upon me the fruits of the Holy Spirit—love to warm my chilled heart, joy to uplift my weary spirit, peace to guard my anxious thoughts, patience to endure this trial, kindness to myself and others, goodness to renew my purpose, faithfulness to hold fast to You, gentleness to soften my burdens, and self-control to reclaim what despair has stolen.

I entrust my sadness into Your Sacred Heart, believing that You who descended into the depths of human suffering will lead me out of this valley and into the sunlight of Your grace. May my life become a living testimony of Your healing love.

And finally, I place my wounded heart beneath the mantle of the Blessed Virgin Mary, Mother of Hope and Refuge of Sinners. As she carried the light of Christ through the darkest days of Good Friday, may she now walk beside me, guiding me always toward her Divine Son. Through her Immaculate Heart, may light break forth in my darkness, and may hope rise anew in my soul.

We ask this through Christ our Lord, the Resurrection and the Life,

   and by the prayers of His most holy Mother, Mary ever

Virgin,
Queen of Angels and Morning Star of Consolation.
Amen.

15

Gratitude for Emotional Wholeness

"The Lord is close to the brokenhearted; He rescues those who are crushed in spirit."
— Psalm 34:18

Gracious Lord Jesus Christ,

Divine Physician of souls and Giver of all consolation, I humbly come before You with a heart overflowing in gratitude. I thank You from the depths of my being for hearing my cries and answering my prayers for emotional healing. Though I still carry the scars of past wounds, I rejoice in the progress You have made within my soul—testaments to Your mercy and love.

You, O Lord, have been faithful even when I could not see the path ahead. Thank You for replacing fear with courage, sadness with hope, despair with peace, and brokenness with a growing sense of wholeness. You have reminded me again and again that I am never alone—that even in the darkest valleys, You walk beside me, guiding me toward the light of Your countenance.

I bless Your holy name for teaching me to lean on You, the true Vine, and to find strength not in myself alone, but in the power of Your grace. In every tear shed and every burden carried, You have drawn near, binding up what was wounded and restoring what was lost.

As I continue to grow in faith and surrender, I ask that You make me a vessel of Your love and healing for others who are hurting. May my life reflect Your compassion, my words bring comfort, and my witness inspire hope. Use my story, once marked by pain, now transformed by grace, to bring glory to Your holy name.

To You be all praise, honor, and glory forever and ever, together with the Father and the Holy Spirit, one God, world without end.

And finally, I entrust my journey of healing and gratitude into the Immaculate Heart of Mary, Mother of Divine Mercy and Comforter of the Afflicted. As she pondered all things in her heart and trusted fully in God's promises, may she intercede for me and lead me always closer to her Son, the source of all healing and joy.

We give You thanks through Christ our Lord,
    and by the prayers of His most holy Mother, Mary ever Virgin,
    Queen of Peace and Advocate of All Who Suffer.
    Amen.

IV

Prayers for Healing of Relationships

16

Healing Marital Bonds

"What therefore God has joined together, let no man separate."
— Matthew 19:6

Lord Jesus Christ,

Divine Bridegroom of souls and Author of all love, I humbly lift up my marriage to You, the sacred covenant You instituted as a reflection of Your own faithful love for the Church. I entrust our union into Your Sacred Heart, asking for Your grace to heal every wound, restore every rift, and renew the joy that sin and hardship may have diminished.

O Lord, where there has been hurt, bring mercy; where there has been misunderstanding, grant clarity; where there has been distance, draw our hearts closer together. Soften both of our hearts toward one another, and help us to see each other not through the eyes of judgment or past pain, but through the lens of Your compassion and truth.

Restore the intimacy we once knew and deepen it beyond what we have known before. Teach us to communicate with patience, to listen with humility, to speak with kindness, and to forgive with generosity. Let charity be the foundation of our home, and let Your peace dwell within our walls.

Strengthen our commitment to honor and cherish one another in sickness and in health, in plenty and in want, until death do us part. May we grow not only older together, but holier together—helping each other reach heaven by word, deed, and mutual support.

Bind us together with cords of divine love that no trial may unravel, and let our home become a domestic sanctuary of faith, joy, and service. Make us living witnesses of Your covenant love, so that others may come to know the beauty of Christian marriage through our lives.

And finally, I entrust our journey as spouses into the Immaculate Heart of Mary, Mother of the Church and Queen of All Families. As she nurtured the Holy Family with purity, devotion, and grace, may she intercede for us, guiding our hearts ever closer to her Divine Son. Through her maternal care, may our love grow deeper, our unity stronger, and our home a true reflection of heaven on earth.

We ask this through Christ our Lord, the sure foundation of every holy vocation,

and by the prayers of His most holy Mother, Mary ever Virgin,

and of St. Joseph, Guardian of the Holy Family.

Amen.

17

Reconciliation with Family Members

"Behold, how good and pleasant it is when brothers dwell in unity!"
— **Psalm 133:1**

Heavenly Father,

God of mercy, harmony, and divine order, I humbly come before You burdened by the brokenness within my family. Whether it be tension with siblings, estrangement from parents, or discord among extended relatives, I lift up these wounds to Your healing presence. With faith in Your power to mend what is torn, I ask that You pour forth Your grace upon our household.

O Lord, remove every wall built by resentment, pride, misunderstanding, or past hurts. Tear down the barriers that have divided us and replace them with bridges of love, forgiveness, compassion, and understanding. Heal the memories that sting, soften hardened hearts, and open minds to reconciliation rooted in truth and charity.

Remind us all, dear Father, that we are united not only by blood but by Your divine purpose—that our family is called to be more than a gathering of individuals, but a reflection of Your love and a domestic church where faith, hope, and charity dwell.

Pour out Your Holy Spirit upon us, that we may live as instruments of peace in one another's lives. Teach us to bear with one another in love, to forgive as You have forgiven us, and to support each other in times of joy and sorrow alike. Let patience, kindness, and humility mark our words and actions, so that we may walk together in harmony according to Your will.

May our family become a living testimony of Your reconciling love—a sign of hope in a world longing for unity. Where there has been division, plant unity; where there has been bitterness, sow mercy; where there has been silence, raise up communication filled with grace.

And finally, I entrust my entire family into the Immaculate Heart of Mary, Mother of Mercy and Queen of Families. As she nurtured the Holy Family with tenderness and faith, may she intercede for us and lead us ever closer to her Divine Son. Through her maternal care, may love grow deeper, wounds find healing, and peace dwell in our home now and always.

We ask this through Christ our Lord, the Prince of Peace,
    and by the prayers of His most holy Mother, Mary ever Virgin,

and of St. Joseph, Guardian of the Holy Family.

Amen.

18

Restoring Parent-Child Relationships

"Fathers, do not provoke your children to anger, but bring them up in the discipline and instruction of the Lord."
— Ephesians 6:4

Merciful Lord Jesus Christ,

Divine Teacher and Model of all holiness, I humbly bring before You the sacred bond between parent and child—a relationship wounded by anger, neglect, miscommunication, or unmet expectations. With heartfelt trust in Your healing power, I ask that You mend what has been broken and restore harmony where there has been division.

O Lord, touch the hearts of both parent and child. Heal their wounds, soften their attitudes toward one another, and open their eyes to see each other through the lens of Your mercy and truth. Where pride has hardened hearts, grant humility; where pain has built walls, pour out forgiveness; where misunderstanding has caused distance, send clarity and compassion.

To parents, O God, grant wisdom and gentleness in guiding their children—not with harshness or control, but with love, patience, and encouragement. Teach them to lead with grace, nurturing their children not only in body and mind, but especially in faith and virtue.

To children, give understanding and respect for the sacrifices made on their behalf, even when imperfectly expressed. Soften rebellious hearts and awaken gratitude for the gift of life and the care—however flawed—that has been given.

Break every cycle of hurt, dysfunction, and estrangement, and replace it with the healing balm of reconciliation and mutual love. Let this bond be renewed in Christ, grounded in prayer, strengthened by forgiveness, and nourished by shared faith.

May the relationship between parent and child become a living reflection of Your unconditional love, O Eternal Father, who never ceases to care for Your children. May homes be filled with peace, joy, and the presence of Your Holy Spirit, so that families may grow together in holiness and walk united toward eternal life.

And finally, I entrust all parents and children into the Immaculate Heart of Mary, Mother of All Families and Queen of Peace. As she lovingly raised You, dear Jesus, with tenderness and devotion, may she intercede for families everywhere, drawing them ever closer to her Divine Son. Through her maternal care, may love flourish, wounds be healed, and homes become true sanctuaries of grace.

We ask this through Christ our Lord, the Way, the Truth, and the Life,
   and by the prayers of His most holy Mother, Mary ever Virgin,
   and of St. Joseph, Guardian of the Holy Family.
   Amen.

19

Mending Broken Friendships

"A faithful friend is a sturdy shelter; he who finds one has found a treasure."
— Sirach 6:14

Faithful God,

Lord of mercy and Source of all love, I humbly bring before You a friendship that has been wounded by betrayal, gossip, misunderstanding, or neglect. Though the distance between us feels vast and reconciliation seems beyond reach, I place my trust in Your power to heal even the deepest wounds and restore what sin and pain have taken away.

O Lord Jesus, Divine Physician of souls, touch both hearts involved in this broken relationship. Heal the hurt that lingers, soften pride where it has hardened, and open minds and hearts to the grace of forgiveness. If bitterness has taken root in the other's soul, loosen its grip; if distrust remains, replace it with hope; if affection has faded, rekindle it with the fire of Your

Holy Spirit.

Grant me, O Lord, the humility and courage to take the first step toward healing—to reach out not with accusation, but with love; not with blame, but with mercy. Teach me to forgive as I have been forgiven, and to seek reconciliation not for my own comfort alone, but for the glory of Your name and the building up of Your Kingdom of love.

If restoration is Your will, guide our steps so that we may walk together once more in peace, bound not only by human affection but by the stronger bond of Christ's charity. Let this friendship become an occasion of grace, drawing both of us closer to You and teaching us the meaning of true companionship rooted in Your eternal love.

And finally, I entrust this fragile relationship into the Immaculate Heart of Mary, Mother of Mercy and Refuge of Sinners. As she stood at the foot of the Cross, united in sorrow and love, may she intercede for us and lead us always back to her Divine Son. Through her maternal care, may wounded friendships be healed, divisions be overcome, and charity flourish anew.

We ask this through Christ our Lord, the Prince of Peace,
    and by the prayers of His most holy Mother, Mary ever Virgin,
    Queen of All Hearts and Model of Perfect Love.
    Amen.

20

Healing Estranged Relationships

For where two or three are gathered in My name, there am I among them."
— Matthew 18:20

Loving Savior,

Divine Healer of broken hearts and Restorer of unity, I come before You with sorrow and hope, lifting up to Your merciful gaze those dear ones from whom I have become estranged. Whether through painful arguments, long years of silence, or wounds too deep to name, the distance between us has left a void that only Your grace can fill.

O Lord, my soul aches at this separation. I entrust every strained relationship into Your Sacred Heart, asking that You bridge the gap that now divides us. Create opportunities for healing, open doors where they seem closed, and guide our steps toward reconciliation if it be according to Your holy will.

Soften every heart that has grown hardened, melt away pride that stands as a wall between souls made for love, and replace bitterness with mercy, silence with truth, and pain with peace.

If reunion is not yet possible, or if wounds remain too fresh, grant me the grace to forgive freely, just as You have forgiven me. Help me to release these loved ones into Your hands, trusting that You continue to work in their lives even when I cannot.

May Your divine love overcome every obstacle, heal every wound, and bring restoration where human effort falls short. Teach me patience in waiting, courage in reaching out, and humility in letting go. Let no relationship be lost to despair, but may all things be redeemed by the power of Your Cross.

And finally, I entrust every estranged bond into the Immaculate Heart of Mary, Mother of Mercy and Queen of Peace. As she stood beneath the Cross, offering her sorrow to God with faith and love, may she intercede for us, drawing us ever closer to her Divine Son. Through her maternal care, may reconciliation blossom, forgiveness flow, and love triumph over every division.

We ask this through Christ our Lord, the Way, the Truth, and the Life,
    and by the prayers of His most holy Mother, Mary ever Virgin,
    Queen of All Hearts and Advocate of Those Who Suffer.

Amen.

21

Invoking Divine Love in All Relationships

"Love one another as I have loved you."
— John 15:12

Gracious and Eternal Father,

Fountain of all love and Source of every good gift, I humbly invite You to pour forth Your divine love into every relationship in my life. Let Your grace transform how I relate to my spouse, family members, friends, coworkers, neighbors, and all whom You place upon my path.

O Lord Jesus Christ, Divine Model of perfect love, teach me and all who are dear to me to love not only in word but in truth and action. Guide us to forgive freely, just as we have been forgiven; to serve selflessly, following Your own example of humility and charity; and to honor one another with kindness, patience, and respect.

Root out from our hearts every trace of jealousy, envy, pride, and selfishness, which so often poison human bonds. Replace these with unity, joy, and mutual edification, that we may build one another up in faith, hope, and love.

May every relationship I am part of be founded on the rock of Your eternal love—the love that is patient, kind, and enduring; the love that bears all things, believes all things, hopes all things, endures all things. Let this love be the light that guides our words, the strength behind our actions, and the peace that sustains us through every season.

I ask, O Lord, that others may see Your light shining through me—that my life may become a reflection of Your goodness, drawing hearts closer to You. May my love for others not be merely human, but supernatural—born of grace, sustained by prayer, and perfected by sacrifice.

And finally, I entrust all my relationships into the Immaculate Heart of Mary, Mother of Charity and Queen of All Hearts. As she lived in perfect union with God and neighbor, may she intercede for me and all those I love, leading us always closer to her Divine Son. Through her maternal care, may charity flourish among us, divisions be healed, and peace dwell in every home.

We ask this through Christ our Lord, the Way, the Truth, and the Life,
    and by the prayers of His most holy Mother, Mary ever

Virgin,
Queen of Apostles and Mirror of All Virtues.

Amen.

22

Thanksgiving for Reconciliation

"How good and pleasant it is when brothers dwell in unity!"
— Psalm 133:1

Almighty and Eternal God,

Lord of mercy, grace, and divine reconciliation, I humbly come before You with a heart overflowing in gratitude. I thank You for hearing my prayers and working miracles in my relationships—miracles that only Your hand could accomplish. You, who are rich in compassion and slow to anger, have softened hearts that were once hardened, opened doors of communication that had been shut, and restored what was broken and lost.

I rejoice in the peace that now dwells among us, a peace that surpasses all understanding and flows from the triumph of Your Cross. Thank You for teaching me, often through pain and patience, the virtues of humility, forgiveness, and perseverance. In healing these relationships, You have not only brought restoration to my life but have also drawn me closer to Your Sacred Heart.

O Lord, as I move forward into this new season of harmony, grant me the grace to nurture these renewed bonds with love, care, and intentionality. Help me to guard against old wounds returning, and teach me to walk always in charity, bearing with one another in gentleness and truth.

Let every healed relationship become a living testimony to Your power, a sign of hope in a world longing for unity, and a reflection of the communion that exists between the Father, the Son, and the Holy Spirit.

To You be all glory, honor, and praise, now and forever, together with the Father and the Holy Spirit, one God, world without end.

And finally, I entrust all my relationships into the Immaculate Heart of Mary, Mother of Divine Mercy and Advocate of All Who Suffer. As she pondered all things in her heart and trusted in God's promises, may she continue to intercede for me and all those I love, leading us always closer to her Divine Son. Through her maternal care, may peace endure, love flourish, and unity be preserved in every bond You have restored.

We give You thanks through Christ our Lord,
    and by the prayers of His most holy Mother, Mary ever Virgin,
        Queen of All Hearts and Mirror of Justice.

V

Prayers for Physical Healing

23

General Physical Healing

"He Himself bore our sins in His body on the cross, so that we might die to sin and live to righteousness; by His wounds you have been healed."
— 1 Peter 2:24

Lord Jesus Christ,

Divine Physician of souls and bodies, Fountain of mercy and Source of all healing, I humbly come before You with a heart full of trust. You alone are the healer of every wound, the restorer of life, and the light that shines even in the darkest hour of suffering.

I surrender to Your sacred and merciful Heart all my pain— whether it afflicts my body, my mind, or my spirit. Every ache, every weakness, every burden I carry, I place into Your wounded hands, knowing that no illness is beyond Your power to heal.

If it be according to Your holy will, O Lord, restore me to full health and vitality. Let Your grace perfect what is lacking in my flesh, and renew my strength from within. In times of trial, deepen my faith and teach me to trust more fully in Your providence. Remind me gently but surely that even in suffering, You are with me—close beside me, holding me in love.

Use this experience of infirmity, Lord, to draw me closer to You, to purify my heart, and to glorify Your holy name. May my life, whether in sickness or in health, be a living witness to Your compassion and truth.

Surround me with the protection of Your holy angels, especially St. Raphael, the healer sent by God to guide and restore, and St. Michael, defender of the sick and afflicted. Guide the hands of those who care for me—doctors, nurses, therapists, and loved ones—that they may be instruments of Your healing grace.

I unite my sufferings to Yours upon the Cross, offering them with You, through You, and in You for the salvation of souls and the glory of the Father's kingdom.

And finally, I entrust my entire journey of healing into the Immaculate Heart of Mary, Mother of Mercy and Health of the Sick. As she once cradled You, the Divine Healer, in her arms, may she now wrap me in her maternal protection and lead me always closer to her Son. Through her intercession, may peace flow into my body, joy into my soul, and hope into every moment of my life.

We ask this through Christ our Lord, the Resurrection and the Life,

and by the prayers of His most holy Mother, Mary ever Virgin,

Queen of Angels and Refuge of Sinners.

Amen.

24

Healing from Chronic Illness

"My grace is sufficient for you, for My power is made perfect in weakness."
— **2 Corinthians 12:9**

Merciful Father,

God of infinite compassion and healer of body and soul, I come before You weighed down by the burden of chronic illness. This affliction has worn upon my body, tested my spirit, and often left me weary beyond words. Yet even now, in the midst of this long and difficult journey, I place my hope in You—for nothing is impossible with God.

O Lord Jesus Christ, Divine Physician of our souls and bodies, I lift up to You every symptom, every limitation, every moment of discouragement. If it be according to Your holy will, heal me—whether through miraculous intervention or through the slow but sure restoration of my strength. In either way, let Your grace be made perfect in my weakness.

Grant me, O Lord, the gift of patience as I walk this path, and the courage to persevere when healing seems far off. Teach me to find joy in small mercies, purpose in suffering, and meaning in moments that feel empty. Let no day pass without some glimpse of Your love, some whisper of hope, some assurance that I am never alone.

Fill me with that peace which surpasses all understanding—a peace that guards my heart and mind in Christ Jesus. Remind me again and again that my worth is not measured by health or ability, but by the depth of Your love, which holds me always in Your sacred Heart.

And finally, I entrust my entire journey into the Immaculate Heart of Mary, Mother of Mercy and Health of the Sick. As she appeared at Lourdes, bringing healing to the afflicted, may she now wrap me in her maternal care and lead me ever closer to her Divine Son. Through her intercession, may light break forth in my darkness, strength rise from my weakness, and holiness grow within my soul.

We ask this through Christ our Lord, the Resurrection and the Life,
   and by the prayers of His most holy Mother, Mary ever Virgin,
      Queen of All Saints and Comforter of the Afflicted.

Amen.

25

Strength During Surgery or Medical Procedures

"God is our refuge and strength, a very present help in trouble."
— **Psalm 46:1**

Gracious Lord Jesus Christ,

Divine Physician of souls and bodies, Eternal Shepherd of my soul, I come before You in humility and trust as I prepare to undergo surgery and enter into this time of medical care. Though fear may stir within me, I choose to place my life entirely in Your wounded hands, knowing that You hold every moment of my existence in love.

O Lord, calm my anxieties and quiet the storms of worry that rise within my heart. Reassure me of Your constant presence—even in the operating room, even in the silence before anesthesia, even in the pain that follows. Let no darkness be untouched by Your light, and let no fear have dominion over me, for I belong to You.

I ask for Your divine protection throughout this entire process. Guard me from complications, shield me from harm, and preserve my life according to Your holy will. Guide the hands and minds of the medical team entrusted with my care, that they may act with wisdom, skill, and compassion as instruments of Your healing grace.

Whether the outcome aligns with my hopes or calls for deeper surrender, I place my confidence in Your sovereign plan. Give me courage to face whatever lies ahead, knowing that You are not only with me—but that You are working all things together for my good and for the glory of Your name.

And finally, I entrust my body, my spirit, and my future into the Immaculate Heart of Mary, Mother of Mercy and Health of the Sick. As she stood faithfully beneath the Cross, may she now wrap me in her maternal protection and lead me always closer to her Divine Son. Through her intercession, may peace guard my heart, hope sustain my soul, and faith uphold my steps.

We ask this through Christ our Lord, the Resurrection and the Life,
    and by the prayers of His most holy Mother, Mary ever Virgin,
    Queen of Angels and Refuge of Sinners.

Amen.

26

Healing for Children

"Truly I tell you, unless you change and become like children, you will never enter the kingdom of heaven."
— Matthew 18:3

Loving Father,

Eternal God and Creator of all life, I humbly bring before You this beloved child who suffers in body and spirit. You formed them in secret, knitting them together in their mother's womb, and called them into existence by name. They are fearfully and wonderfully made in Your image and likeness, and I entrust their fragile body and precious soul into Your most tender care.

O Lord Jesus Christ, Divine Physician of children and healer of every wound, I ask that You stretch forth Your hand in mercy and touch this child with the power of Your love. Strengthen their immune system, restore their health, and calm every fear that stirs within their heart. Let no pain be without purpose, and let no suffering go unheld in Your sacred embrace.

Surround them with Your angels of protection and peace, especially St. Michael the Archangel, their guardian against evil, and St. Raphael the Archangel, the divine healer sent to guide and restore. Guide the hands and minds of the doctors, nurses, and caregivers who tend to them, that they may act as instruments of Your healing grace.

Pour forth upon this child the gifts of the Holy Spirit—wisdom, understanding, courage, and hope—that they may grow not only in strength and health, but also in faith, joy, and holiness. May they come to know Your love early, walk in Your ways, and live always under the watchful gaze of Heaven.

And finally, I place this child beneath the mantle of the Blessed Virgin Mary, Mother of Mercy and Health of the Sick. As she lovingly cared for the Child Jesus, may she now wrap this little one in her maternal protection and lead them safely into the arms of her Divine Son. Through her intercession, may healing flow, fears be calmed, and perfect love cast out all distress.

We ask this through Christ our Lord, the Good Shepherd and Savior of little children,

and by the prayers of His most holy Mother, Mary ever Virgin,

Queen of Angels and Refuge of Little Ones.

Amen.

27

Healing from Pain and Suffering

"The Lord is near to the brokenhearted and rescues those who are crushed in spirit."
— Psalm 34:18

Compassionate Savior,

Divine Healer of wounded souls and Victim of Love upon the Cross, I come before You weighed down by pain that seems too great to bear. My body may ache, my heart may bleed, and my spirit may tremble—but I know that You understand. You, who bore the weight of all sin and sorrow, have walked the path of suffering before me and now walk beside me still.

In Your boundless mercy, O Jesus, relieve this anguish and grant me moments of peace, even if only glimpses of Your healing presence. If it be according to Your holy will, ease this burden and shorten the night of trial. But if I must continue along this road, grant me strength equal to my need and grace sufficient for every step.

Teach me, dear Lord, to unite my suffering to Yours upon Calvary, offering it with love for the salvation of souls and the glory of Your name. Let my pain become a hidden act of worship, a silent hymn of trust, and a source of spiritual fruitfulness for others. May it be redemptive, joined to Your own sacrifice on the altar of the Cross.

Replace my discomfort with the balm of Your consolation, my fear with the light of Your truth, and my sorrow with the joy that comes from knowing I am never alone. Let Your peace, which surpasses all understanding, guard my heart and mind in Christ Jesus.

I place my complete trust in You, knowing that no trial will ever separate me from Your love. You are near to the brokenhearted; You do not despise our wounds but sanctify them. Hold me close in this time of need, and let Your grace perfect what is weak in me.

And finally, I entrust my suffering into the Immaculate Heart of Mary, Mother of Sorrows and Refuge of Sinners. As she stood beneath the Cross, sharing in Your passion with faith and love, may she now wrap me in her maternal care and lead me always closer to her Divine Son. Through her intercession, may my heart be united more fully to Yours and my life become a living witness of hope.

We ask this through Christ our Lord, the Suffering Servant who brings healing to the world,
   and by the prayers of His most holy Mother, Mary ever Virgin,

Queen of Martyrs and Comforter of the Afflicted.

Amen

28

Healing for the Elderly

"Even to your old age I am He, and to gray hairs I will carry you. I have made, and I will bear; I will carry and will save."
— Isaiah 46:4

Faithful God,

Eternal Father and Shepherd of all generations, I lift up to You the beloved elderly among us—those who have walked long paths of labor, love, and sacrifice. As their bodies grow weaker and the burdens of age press more heavily upon them, uphold them with the strength of Your mighty hand and remind them that they are never forgotten in Your sight.

O Lord Jesus Christ, Divine Physician of soul and body, look with mercy upon those whose steps falter and whose hands tremble. Protect them from illness, falls, and accidents. Grant them dignity in frailty, peace in uncertainty, and joy in the knowledge that their lives continue to bear great worth in Your eyes.

Surround them with angels of protection and consolation, especially their Guardian Angels, and bless those who care for them—nurses, family members, and caregivers—with abundant patience, compassion, and strength. Let every act of kindness offered to them be a hidden offering of love to You, and reward it a hundredfold in Your Kingdom.

Fill their days with small mercies and moments of grace. May they find comfort in the sacraments, strength in prayer, and hope in the promise of eternal life. Remind them—and all of us—that though the body may weaken, the soul is ever renewed, and death is not an end but a beginning.

And finally, I entrust all our beloved elders into the Immaculate Heart of Mary, Mother of Mercy and Queen of All Saints. As she lovingly cared for the aged Simeon and Anna in the Temple, may she now wrap our elderly loved ones in her maternal protection and lead them ever closer to her Divine Son. Through her intercession, may joy rise in their hearts, peace dwell in their homes, and faith sustain them to the very end.

We ask this through Christ our Lord, the Resurrection and the Life,
    and by the prayers of His most holy Mother, Mary ever Virgin,
    Queen of Heaven and Mother of the Eternal Covenant.

    Amen.

29

Thanksgiving for Healing

"Give thanks to the Lord, for He is good; His mercy endures forever."
— Psalm 107:1

Gracious Lord Jesus Christ,

Eternal High Priest and Divine Physician of soul and body, I humbly come before You with a heart overflowing in gratitude. I thank You for hearing my prayers and answering them according to Your holy will—not always as I expected, but always as I needed. Whether my healing came swiftly like a rushing river or gradually like the rising sun, I rejoice in Your unfailing goodness and boundless mercy.

I bless Your holy name for restoring what was broken, renewing what had grown weak, and breathing new life into what once seemed lost. In Your compassion, You have lifted me from the dust and set my feet upon a rock, making my steps secure (Psalm 40:2). Every wound You have touched, every sorrow You have borne, and every tear You have gathered—you have not forgotten one.

Thank You for filling my heart with peace that surpasses all understanding, and for surrounding me with the warmth of Your love when I could find no comfort elsewhere. Now, having tasted Your healing power, I desire to share my testimony with others, that they too may come to know Your saving grace and place their trust in You.

May my life become a living hymn of praise—a daily offering of thanksgiving for all that You have done. Let every healed relationship, every restored strength, and every answered prayer point someone else toward Your Sacred Heart.

And finally, I entrust my journey of healing and gratitude into the Immaculate Heart of Mary, Mother of Mercy and Queen of All Saints. As she rejoiced at the wedding feast of Cana and stood faithfully beneath the Cross, may she now lead me always closer to her Divine Son. Through her intercession, may my heart continue to grow in faith, hope, and charity, bearing lasting fruit for the Kingdom of God.

We give You thanks through Christ our Lord,
    and by the prayers of His most holy Mother, Mary ever Virgin,
    Queen of Heaven and Mirror of All Holiness.

Amen

VI

Prayers for Healthy Finances

30

Breaking Generational Poverty

"Seek first the kingdom of God and His righteousness, and all these things will be added to you."
— Matthew 6:33

Almighty Father,

Eternal and bountiful God, source of every good gift and fountain of all blessings, I humbly come before You to renounce every generational pattern of poverty, lack, and scarcity that has held my family line in bondage. By the saving power of the Cross and the precious Blood of Your Son, Jesus Christ, I break every chain of material and spiritual destitution that has hindered abundance, dignity, and freedom in our lives.

O Lord of hosts and Provider of all good things, I proclaim with faith that no curse has power over those who belong to Your household. Shatter the cycles of poverty that have oppressed my ancestors, and pour forth Your blessings abundantly upon me and my descendants. Grant us the grace to walk in faith, not fear; in trust, not anxiety; knowing that You are our heavenly Father who clothes the lilies of the field and feeds the birds of the air.

Teach me, O Lord, to steward all that You entrust to me—time, talent, and treasure—with wisdom, justice, and generosity. Open the windows of heaven, as You promised through the prophet Malachi, and let Your blessings overflow so that there shall not be room enough to receive them (Malachi 3:10).

May this breakthrough in my life bring glory to Your holy name and become a channel of blessing for future generations. Let my home be marked by integrity, my labor be fruitful, and my table always full with bread enough for today and hope for tomorrow.

And finally, I entrust my entire family into the Immaculate Heart of Mary, Mother of Divine Providence and Queen of the Holy Family. As she cared for the needs of Jesus and St. Joseph in Nazareth, may she now intercede for us, guiding our steps and leading us always closer to her Divine Son. Through her maternal care, may poverty give way to plenty, despair to hope, and scarcity to abundance poured out by Your loving hand.

We ask this through Christ our Lord, the Bread of Life and Shepherd of the Poor,
    and by the prayers of His most holy Mother, Mary ever Virgin,

31

Provision During Hardship

"The Lord will provide for all the needs of His faithful ones."
— Psalm 145:19 (adapted)

Heavenly Father,

Eternal God and Shepherd of my soul, I humbly bring before You my financial struggles and the burdens that weigh heavily upon my heart. In moments of anxiety and uncertainty—when debt presses down like a heavy yoke and tomorrow seems unclear—I call upon You, who are "The Lord Who Provides," and place my trust in Your unfailing care.

You, O Lord, are the owner of every mountain, the master of every harvest, and the provider of every good gift. As it is written, "The cattle on a thousand hills are Mine" (Psalm 50:10), and nothing is beyond Your loving providence. When fear rises within me, remind me that I serve a God who feeds the birds of the air and clothes the lilies of the field—how much more will He care for His beloved children?

O Lord Jesus Christ, Divine Worker of Nazareth and Bread of Life, open doors of opportunity where none seem to exist. Bless the work of my hands, grant wisdom in my decisions, and multiply even the smallest efforts according to Your holy will. Teach me to manage resources with integrity and generosity, ever mindful that all I have comes from You and is meant to serve Your Kingdom.

Replace my anxiety with unwavering trust, my worry with deep confidence in Your abundant provision. Free me from the idolatry of wealth and anchor my soul in the riches of grace. Let this season of trial become a school of faith, where I learn to depend not on worldly security, but on You alone—the true source of every blessing.

Provide for all my needs, O Father, according to the riches of Your glory in Christ Jesus (Philippians 4:19). Sustain my household, feed my family, and give me the grace to walk each day in peace, knowing that no one who hopes in You shall ever be abandoned.

And finally, I entrust my livelihood and daily bread into the Immaculate Heart of Mary, Mother of Divine Providence and Queen of the Holy Family. As she cared for the needs of Jesus and St. Joseph in Nazareth, may she now intercede for me, guiding my steps and leading me always closer to her Divine Son. Through her maternal care, may poverty give way to plenty, fear to hope, and scarcity to abundance poured out by Your loving hand.

We ask this through Christ our Lord, the Way, the Truth, and the Life,

and by the prayers of His most holy Mother, Mary ever Virgin,

Queen of Families and Mirror of All Holiness.

Amen

32

Freedom from Debt

No one can serve two masters... You cannot serve God and money."
— Matthew 6:24

Lord of All,

Eternal King and Master of every heart, I humbly come before You weighed down by the burden of debt that clings to me like a heavy yoke. I confess the stress, the shame, and the fear that often accompany this struggle, and I ask for Your mercy, wisdom, and grace to overcome it.

O Lord Jesus Christ, Divine Worker of Nazareth and Bread of Life, be my strength and my guide. Show me the practical steps I must take to reduce my obligations, and grant me the discipline and prudence to live within the means You provide. Open doors where they seem closed, bless the work of my hands, and multiply even the smallest efforts according to Your holy will.

Break the chains of financial bondage that threaten my peace and cloud my joy. Free me from anxiety, restore order to my finances, and lead me into the light of Your providence. Teach me to manage what You entrust to me with integrity, generosity, and humility, always mindful that all things belong to You.

Help me, O Lord, to honor You not only with my offerings but with my choices—to seek first Your kingdom above earthly security, and to place my trust not in riches, which are fleeting, but in You, who are eternal. Let me live not for the abundance of possessions, but for the richness of Your love and the treasures laid up in heaven.

Let my heart remain steadfast in gratitude, even in times of want, knowing that true wealth lies not in what I own, but in the depth of my relationship with You. May I never lose sight of the greater inheritance that awaits all who hope in Christ.

And finally, I entrust my financial burdens into the Immaculate Heart of Mary, Mother of Divine Providence and Queen of the Holy Family. As she cared for the needs of her Son and Saint Joseph in Nazareth, may she now intercede for me, guiding my steps and leading me always closer to her Divine Son. Through her maternal care, may poverty give way to sufficiency, despair to hope, and debt to freedom in Christ.

We ask this through Christ our Lord, the Way, the Truth, and the Life,
   and by the prayers of His most holy Mother, Mary ever Virgin,
   Queen of Families and Mirror of All Holiness.

33

Wisdom in Business and Work

"Whatever you do, work at it with all your heart, as for the Lord rather than for men."
— Colossians 3:23

Sovereign God,

Eternal Father and Lord of all creation, I humbly come before You to consecrate my work and business endeavors to Your divine will. In every decision, in every task, and in every responsibility, I ask for the gift of heavenly wisdom—that my labors may reflect not only skill, but holiness; not only success, but integrity.

O Lord Jesus Christ, Divine Worker of Nazareth and Master of All Trades, be present in my place of employment, my profession, or my enterprise. Guide my hands, enlighten my mind, and purify my intentions so that everything I do may align with Your purposes and bring glory to Your holy name.

Bless the fruits of my labor, O Lord, and multiply them according to Your mercy. Let honesty be my foundation, diligence my discipline, and justice my standard. Protect me from dishonesty, exploitation, and greed, and teach me to serve others through my work—not seeking only profit, but purpose; not only advancement, but virtue.

If I face unemployment, uncertainty, or career challenges, lead me by Your grace to opportunities that fulfill both my earthly needs and the higher calling You have placed upon my life. Open doors that no man can shut, and grant me the courage to walk through them with faith and integrity.

May I always remember that I am a steward of the gifts You have entrusted to me—my talents, time, and treasures. Help me to use them wisely, generously, and with a heart united to Yours.

And finally, I entrust my vocation and daily work into the Immaculate Heart of Mary, Mother of Divine Wisdom and Queen of All Laborers. As she nurtured You, dear Jesus, and supported Saint Joseph in his work, may she now guide me in humility, perseverance, and service. Through her maternal intercession, may my labor bear fruit for Your Kingdom and my heart remain ever faithful to Your call.

We ask this through Christ our Lord, the King of Kings and Lord of Lords,
    and by the prayers of His most holy Mother, Mary ever Virgin,
    Queen of Apostles and Mirror of All Virtues.

34

Peace Amidst Financial Stress

"Do not be anxious about anything, but in every situation, by prayer and petition, with thanksgiving, present your requests to God. And the peace of God, which transcends all understanding, will guard your hearts and your minds in Christ Jesus."
— **Philippians 4:6–7**

Prince of Peace,

Divine Healer of anxious hearts and Source of all consolation, I come before You weighed down by the burdens of financial worry. The storms of uncertainty rage within me—fears about provision, concerns over debts, and anxieties about the future. Yet I cast all these cares upon You, knowing that You care deeply for me and hold my life in Your loving hands.

O Lord Jesus, quiet the tempests of my soul with the gentle whisper of Your mercy. Replace my fear with faith, my worry with hope, and my anxiety with the perfect peace that only You can give. Teach me to seek first Your kingdom and to trust that all else will be given according to the Father's good pleasure.

Help me to fix my eyes not on the shifting sands of material security, but on the unshakable rock of Your promises. Let my heart remain rooted in what truly matters—my relationship with You, the source of all love, joy, and peace. Guard my mind against despair and doubt, and fill me with confidence in Your divine plan, which is always one of hope and not of harm (Jeremiah 29:11).

Thank You for being my provider, protector, and refuge in every season. In times of plenty, You bless; in times of want, You sustain. Whether my cup runs over or my path grows narrow, I know that You are with me, guiding me by Your rod and staff, leading me beside still waters.

And finally, I entrust my worries into the Immaculate Heart of Mary, Mother of Trust and Queen of Peace. As she pondered all things in her heart and trusted fully in God's promises, may she now wrap me in her maternal comfort and lead me always closer to her Divine Son. Through her intercession, may peace rise in my soul, hope shine in darkness, and joy return to my spirit.

We ask this through Christ our Lord, the Resurrection and the Life,
   and by the prayers of His most holy Mother, Mary ever Virgin,
   Queen of Angels and Refuge of Sinners.

Amen.

35

Generosity and Stewardship

"Each of you should give what you have decided in your heart to give, not reluctantly or under compulsion, for God loves a cheerful giver."
— 2 Corinthians 9:7

Generous Father,

Eternal fountain of all goodness and Giver of every perfect gift, I humbly come before You to offer my heart in gratitude for all that You have bestowed upon me—my life, my talents, and the material blessings I so undeservedly enjoy.

O Lord Jesus Christ, Divine Steward of the Father's Kingdom and Good Shepherd of souls, teach me to be a wise and faithful steward of the gifts You have entrusted to my care. Open my eyes to see the needs around me, and grant me a heart that is quick to give, slow to withhold, and always eager to share.

Protect me from the snares of selfishness and greed, which so easily creep into the human heart. Root out any attachment to earthly riches that might separate me from Your love. Help me to store up treasures not in this passing world, but in heaven, where neither moth nor rust consumes, and where true joy is found (Matthew 6:19–21).

Bless my tithes and offerings, O Lord, and multiply their impact beyond what I can imagine. Let even the smallest act of generosity become a seed of grace, bearing fruit for Your kingdom and bringing relief to those in need. Use my hands as instruments of Your mercy, and let my resources become channels of Your divine providence.

May my generosity reflect the boundless love of Your Sacred Heart—selfless, sacrificial, and poured out for others. Inspire those around me by my example, drawing them closer to Your heart and awakening in them the joy of giving freely for the sake of love.

And finally, I entrust my heart and my resources into the Immaculate Heart of Mary, Mother of Charity and Queen of the Apostles. As she gave all for the coming of the Kingdom, may she teach me to give without counting the cost and to serve without seeking reward. Through her intercession, may my life become a living sacrifice of praise and charity, offered always to Your greater glory.

We ask this through Christ our Lord, the Bread of Life and Master of the Harvest,
    and by the prayers of His most holy Mother, Mary ever Virgin,

Queen of All Saints and Mirror of Perfection.

Amen.

36

Thanksgiving for Financial Provision

"My God will supply all your needs according to His riches in glory in Christ Jesus."
— **Philippians 4:19**

Gracious Provider,

Eternal Father and Fountain of every blessing, I come before You with a heart overflowing in gratitude. I thank You for hearing my prayers and answering them—not always as I expected, but always as I needed. Whether through small mercies that brighten weary days or miraculous provisions that reveal Your mighty hand, I recognize and rejoice in Your constant care.

O Lord Jesus Christ, Divine Steward of the Father's Kingdom and Bread of Life eternal, I bless Your holy name for teaching me to trust in Your unfailing love and for drawing me closer to Your Sacred Heart during seasons of trial and dependence. You have fed me when I was hungry, clothed me when I was in need, and guided me when I could not see the way.

Thank You for reminding me that every good gift comes from above, and that no one who hopes in You shall ever be abandoned. In humility, I acknowledge that all I have is a gift from Your generous hand. Help me to remain ever grateful, and to share freely with others the abundance You bestow upon me, becoming a channel of Your mercy and love.

May my life, my work, and my very breath bring honor to Your holy name, now and for all eternity. Let every blessing received become a reason for praise, an occasion for worship, and a witness to Your saving power.

And finally, I entrust my journey of gratitude into the Immaculate Heart of Mary, Mother of Mercy and Queen of All Saints. As she rejoiced at Cana and pondered all things in her heart, may she now lead me always closer to her Divine Son. Through her intercession, may my heart grow in faith, my hands remain open in generosity, and my soul proclaim with hers: "My spirit rejoices in God my Savior."

We give You thanks through Christ our Lord,
    and by the prayers of His most holy Mother, Mary ever Virgin,
    Queen of Heaven and Mirror of All Holiness.

Amen.

VII

Prayers for Protection and Deliverance

37

Protection from Evil Spirits

"Submit yourselves therefore to God. Resist the devil, and he will flee from you."
— James 4:7

Almighty and Eternal God,

Lord of hosts and King of all creation, I humbly come before You in the name of Your beloved Son, Jesus Christ, to renounce every influence of evil spirits over my life, my soul, my body, and my household. By the authority of Christ crucified and risen, I break every chain of fear, oppression, and spiritual bondage. I reject all works of darkness and sever every tie that binds me to the enemy.

O Lord, fulfill Your promise: "No weapon formed against me

shall prosper" (Isaiah 54:17). Clothe me in the armor of light, shield me with the Precious Blood of Jesus, and surround me with legions of holy angels, especially St. Michael the Archangel, Your chief warrior against the forces of evil.

Drive away every spirit of darkness that seeks to harm me or those I love. Cast into the abyss every demonic presence that has sought to deceive, divide, or destroy. Let no shadow of evil find a foothold in my heart, my home, or my relationships. Break curses, dissolve lies, and silence the voice of the deceiver forevermore.

Fill me, O Lord, with the fire of Your Holy Spirit—light to dispel darkness, truth to overcome deception, and peace to guard my soul. Let Your divine presence dwell within me, making my body a temple of holiness and my home a sanctuary of grace.

I place my complete trust in You, O Lord, my refuge and fortress, my shield and stronghold. In times of danger, You are my protection; in moments of temptation, You are my strength. No evil shall befall me, no plague shall draw near my dwelling, for You command Your angels to guard me in all my ways (Psalm 91:1–13).

And finally, I entrust myself, my loved ones, and my entire household into the Immaculate Heart of Mary, Mother of God and Queen of Angels. As she crushed the head of the serpent by her obedience and faith, may she now wrap me in her mantle of purity and lead me always closer to her Divine Son. Through her maternal intercession, may every door opened to darkness be sealed by the power of the Cross, and may the light of Christ shine unbroken in my life.

We ask this through Christ our Lord, the Conqueror of death and destroyer of the devil,
    and by the prayers of His most holy Mother, Mary ever Virgin,
    Queen of Heaven and Refuge of Sinners.

    Amen

38

Deliverance from Addiction

"If the Son sets you free, you will be free indeed."
— John 8:36

Loving Savior,

Divine Physician of soul and body, I cry out to You from the depths of my suffering. I bring before Your merciful gaze the chains of addiction that bind me—whether to substances, behaviors, or destructive habits—that have taken root in my life and stolen my freedom. In faith, I renounce their power over me and call upon the saving name of Jesus Christ to break every bond.

O Lord, by the wounds You suffered on the Cross, heal what is broken within me. Set me free from the tyranny of sin and the deception of the enemy. Fill the emptiness that once welcomed darkness with the light of Your Holy Spirit. Pour forth the fruits of Your Presence—love to replace selfishness, joy to replace despair, peace to replace chaos, patience to replace impulsivity, kindness to replace cruelty, goodness to replace vice, faithfulness to replace betrayal, gentleness to replace harshness, and self-control to replace compulsion.

Strengthen my resolve to walk the narrow path of holiness. Grant me courage in moments of temptation, wisdom in times of weakness, and perseverance when the road seems long. Surround me with holy companions—those who will walk beside me in truth, support my recovery in love, and point me always back to You.

I ask, O Lord, for the grace to rebuild what has been broken—to restore relationships wounded by my past actions, to reclaim the dignity lost to sin, and to rediscover the purpose You have written on my heart from the beginning.

Thank You for making all things new in Christ Jesus. Thank You for mercy that never ends, for grace sufficient for every need, and for love that refuses to let go.

And finally, I entrust my journey of healing into the Immaculate Heart of Mary, Mother of Mercy and Refuge of Sinners. As she stood beneath the Cross, offering her sorrow to God with faith and love, may she now wrap me in her maternal care and lead me always closer to her Divine Son. Through her intercession, may purity return to my soul, peace dwell in my heart, and freedom rise in my steps.

We ask this through Christ our Lord, the Way, the Truth, and the Life,
    and by the prayers of His most holy Mother, Mary ever

Virgin,
Queen of Apostles and Mirror of All Virtues.

Amen.

39

Deliverance from Sexual Sin

"Flee from immorality. Every other sin which a man commits is outside the body, but the immoral man sins against his own body. Do you not know that your body is a temple of the Holy Spirit within you, whom you have from God?"
— 1 Corinthians 6:18–19

Merciful Lord Jesus Christ,

Divine Physician of souls and Savior of the world, I come before You with a contrite heart, repenting of all sexual sins that have defiled my body—the temple of the Holy Spirit. Whether through lustful thoughts, pornography, adultery, impurity, or any act contrary to Your holy design, I renounce these sins and turn away from every path that leads me away from Your truth.

O Lord of purity and light, cleanse me in the Blood of the Lamb and forgive me by the infinite merits of Your Cross. Heal what is broken within me, renew my heart, and restore my dignity as a child of God. Break every chain of addiction, every stronghold of temptation, and every deception of the enemy that has sought to rob me of chastity, peace, and holiness.

Fill me with the fire of Your Holy Spirit—granting me purity of mind, modesty of heart, and self-mastery according to the law of love. Teach me to honor my body as a sacred vessel of grace and to reverence others as temples of Your presence. If I am married, strengthen my union and restore intimacy to reflect the love between Christ and His Church. If I am single, grant me patience, virtue, and the grace to wait upon Your timing and wisdom.

Let my thoughts be transformed by the Gospel, my desires shaped by virtue, and my actions rooted in righteousness. May I walk each day in the freedom You won for me on the Cross— no longer enslaved to sin, but alive to righteousness, clothed in the new self created in holiness and truth (Ephesians 4:24).

And finally, I entrust my journey of healing into the Immaculate Heart of Mary, Mother of Purity and Refuge of Sinners. As she lived in perfect integrity and was overshadowed by the Holy Spirit, may she now wrap me in her maternal protection and lead me always closer to her Divine Son. Through her intercession, may chastity return to my soul, holiness rise in my steps, and grace triumph over every weakness.

We ask this through Christ our Lord, the Way, the Truth, and the Life,

    and by the prayers of His most holy Mother, Mary ever Virgin,

    Queen of All Hearts and Mirror of Purity.

40

Breaking Bondages of the Past

"Therefore, if anyone is in Christ, he is a new creation. The old has passed away; behold, the new has come."
— 2 Corinthians 5:17

Redeemer God,

Eternal Father of mercy and Lord of all healing, I humbly come before You to lay at the foot of the Cross the heavy burdens of my past—traumas that linger, regrets that haunt, failures that shame, and sins that still cling to my soul. By the saving name of Your Son, Jesus Christ, I renounce every stronghold these memories have held over me, and I declare that no chain from yesterday can bind me today.

O Lord Jesus, Divine Physician of wounded hearts and Victor over sin and death, break every bondage that has kept me enslaved to pain. Heal the deep wounds left by abuse, neglect, rejection, abandonment, or betrayal. Replace every scar with Your love, every emptiness with Your acceptance, and every lie whispered into my soul with the truth written upon my heart: I am fearfully and wonderfully made, chosen, beloved, and redeemed.

Erase the false voices of condemnation, O Lord, and silence the enemy who seeks to remind me of what I once was. Instead, let the voice of the Good Shepherd speak life, freedom, and holiness into every corner of my being. Let Your grace perfect what is broken, and restore the joy of my salvation.

By the power of the Holy Spirit, make me a new creation in Christ. Let the old self—marked by fear, shame, and sorrow—be crucified with Christ, and raise me to walk in the fullness of the abundant life You have prepared for me. Grant me the courage to leave behind what no longer serves Your glory and the faith to embrace the future You promise.

And finally, I entrust my journey of healing and renewal into the Immaculate Heart of Mary, Mother of Mercy and Refuge of Sinners. As she pondered all things in her heart and trusted fully in God's promises, may she now wrap me in her maternal care and lead me always closer to her Divine Son. Through her intercession, may my heart be cleansed, my mind renewed, and my life transformed by the liberating love of Christ.

We ask this through Christ our Lord, the Resurrection and the Life,
    and by the prayers of His most holy Mother, Mary ever Virgin,
    Queen of Peace and Mirror of Justice.

41

Deliverance from Unhealthy Soul Ties

"Do not be bound together with unbelievers. For what partnership has righteousness with lawlessness? Or what fellowship has light with darkness?"
— **2 Corinthians 6:14**

Heavenly Father,

God of holiness and love, I humbly come before You to lay bare the hidden chains that bind my soul—unhealthy soul ties formed through sin, pain, or broken relationships. In the mighty name of Your Son, Jesus Christ, I renounce every connection that does not honor You—those born of sexual immorality, emotional dependency, manipulation, unforgiveness, idolatry, or any union that has led me away from Your will.

O Lord Jesus Christ, Divine Healer and Lover of souls, I call upon You to sever every spiritual, emotional, or physical bond that has held me captive. Break the cords of attachments that do not lead to holiness, and free me from the lingering effects of past relationships that have wounded my spirit, clouded my mind, or compromised my integrity.

Heal the wounds left behind by these entanglements—especially the scars that still ache within my heart. Restore my sense of identity as Your beloved child, made in Your image and called to walk in freedom. Fill the emptiness left by false connections with the fullness of Your presence, that I may no longer seek love where it cannot be found, but rest always in the arms of Your mercy.

Forgive me, O Lord, for any role I played in forming these bonds contrary to Your design. Heal my conscience, renew my heart, and grant me the grace to forgive those who have wounded me. Free me from bitterness, guilt, or shame, and help me release all that has kept me chained to the past.

I ask, dear Lord, that You protect my heart from forming future unhealthy ties. Lead me into relationships that are rooted in truth, built on virtue, and directed toward Your glory. Teach me to love as You love—selflessly, chastely, and with reverence for the dignity of every person.

Thank You for setting me free, for redeeming what was lost, and for restoring my soul to its rightful place beneath the shadow of Your wings. May I live henceforth not for the approval of others, nor under the weight of old chains, but for You alone—my Savior, my Spouse, and my eternal inheritance.

And finally, I entrust my journey of healing and freedom into the Immaculate Heart of Mary, Mother of Purity and Refuge of Sinners. As she lived in perfect consecration to God's will, may she now wrap me in her maternal protection and lead me always closer to her Divine Son. Through her intercession, may my heart be purified, my soul set free, and my life become a living sacrifice of praise.

We ask this through Christ our Lord, the Way, the Truth, and the Life,
   and by the prayers of His most holy Mother, Mary ever Virgin,
   Queen of Peace and Mirror of All Holiness.

   Amen.

42

Prayer for Deliverance from Curses, Hexes, and Witchcraft

"Submit yourselves therefore to God. Resist the devil, and he will flee from you."
— James 4:7

Almighty Father,

Eternal King and Lord of hosts, I humbly come before You clothed in the armor of faith, renouncing every curse, hex, and evil spell that has been cast against me, my family, or anything entrusted to my care. In the mighty name of Your Son, Jesus Christ, I declare that no weapon formed against me shall prosper, and every tongue that rises against me in judgment, I shall condemn (Isaiah 54:17).

O Lord Jesus Christ, Divine Conqueror of death and destroyer of the devil's works, I break every chain, stronghold, and malevolent influence that seeks to harm me. I cancel all pacts, oaths, or agreements made—whether knowingly or unknowingly—with the forces of darkness. I reject every deception, idolatry, or occult practice that has opened the door to evil, and I surrender my entire being completely to Your light, truth, and divine protection.

By the power of the Cross and the Precious Blood of Christ, I command every spirit of witchcraft, divination, sorcery, and false prophecy to depart from my life and never return. I bind these evil forces in the name of Jesus and loose upon my life the fullness of Your blessings, mercy, and peace.

Heal every wound left by these attacks—physical ailments, emotional trauma, or spiritual confusion. Restore what the enemy has stolen, cleanse my soul of any lingering effects of evil, and renew within me a right spirit, filled with holiness, freedom, and joy.

Surround me, O Lord, with legions of holy angels, especially St. Michael the Archangel, chief warrior of heaven, who stands ready to defend Your children. Wrap me in the mantle of Your protection and shield me beneath the wings of Your love.

I thank You, dear Father, for delivering me from the powers of darkness and translating me into the Kingdom of Your beloved Son. I walk not in fear, but in confidence, knowing that greater is He who is in me than he who is in the world (1 John 4:4). By the victory of Christ's resurrection, I am free indeed.

And finally, I entrust my body, soul, and loved ones into the Immaculate Heart of Mary, Mother of God and Queen of Angels. As she crushed the head of the serpent by her obedience and faith, may she now wrap me in her maternal protection and lead me always closer to her Divine Son. Through her intercession, may every door opened to evil be sealed by the power of the Cross, and may the light of Christ shine unbroken in my life.

We ask this through Christ our Lord, the Resurrection and the Life,

and by the prayers of His most holy Mother, Mary ever Virgin,

Queen of Heaven and Refuge of Sinners.

Amen.

43

Thanksgiving for Deliverance

"He has delivered us from the domain of darkness and transferred us to the kingdom of His beloved Son."
— **Colossians 1:13**

Victorious Lord Jesus Christ,

Eternal King and Conqueror of sin and death, I come before You with a heart overflowing in gratitude. I thank You for setting me free from the powers of darkness and transferring me into the Kingdom of Your beloved Son. By the power of the Cross and the merits of Your Precious Blood, You have broken every chain that once held me captive and shattered every stronghold of evil that sought my ruin.

O Lord of hosts, I rejoice in the liberty You have won for me— a freedom not rooted in this world, but in the truth of Your Gospel. I bless Your holy name for rescuing me from the snares of the enemy and leading me into the light of Your presence.

No longer do I walk in fear, for You are my strength, my shield, and my salvation.

I offer You my deepest thanks for every wound healed, every deception unmasked, and every lie silenced by Your Word. You have freed me not only from bondage, but for a new life of grace, holiness, and service. May I never take for granted the price You paid for my redemption, nor grow complacent in the battle for my soul.

Keep me ever vigilant against the schemes of the devil, and grant me the grace to resist temptation with courage and faith. Strengthen my resolve to walk always in the light of Your truth, to reject all that displeases You, and to cling to all that builds up Your Kingdom.

Let my life become a living testimony to Your mighty works, a beacon of hope to those still in chains, and a hymn of praise to Your saving power. May others see the goodness You have done for me and be drawn to seek Your mercy, healing, and freedom for themselves.

And finally, I entrust my journey of continued protection and sanctity into the Immaculate Heart of Mary, Mother of Mercy and Refuge of Sinners. As she stood beneath the Cross, sharing in the victory of her Divine Son, may she now lead me always closer to You. Through her intercession, may my heart remain steadfast in grace, my steps firm in faith, and my soul forever united to Your love.

We give You thanks through Christ our Lord, the Resurrection

and the Life,
   and by the prayers of His most holy Mother, Mary ever
Virgin,
   Queen of Angels and Mirror of All Holiness.

Amen.

VIII

Seeking the Intercession of the Mother of God

44

Salve Regina

Hail, holy Queen, Mother of mercy,
  Our life, our sweetness, and our hope.
  To thee do we cry, poor banished children of Eve;
  To thee do we send up our sighs,
  Mourning and weeping in this valley of tears.
  Turn then, most gracious advocate,
  Thine eyes of mercy toward us,
  And after this, our exile,
  Show unto us the blessed fruit of thy womb, Jesus.
  O clement, O loving, O sweet Virgin Mary!
  Pray for us, O holy Mother of God,
  That we may be made worthy of the promises of Christ.
Amen.

45

The Memorare

Remember, O most gracious Virgin Mary,
   That never was it known
   That anyone who fled to thy protection,
   Implored thy help, or sought thy intercession,
   Was left unaided.
   Inspired by this confidence,
   I fly unto thee, O Virgin of virgins, my Mother.
   To thee do I come,
   Before thee I stand, sinful and sorrowful.
   O Mother of the Word Incarnate,
   Despise not my petitions,
   But in thy mercy hear and answer me. Amen.

46

Ancient Byzantine Prayer to the Theotokos

O Theotokos, Virgin Mary,
You are the true vine that bore the Fruit of Life.
Through you, we have received salvation;
Through you, we have been reconciled to God.
Intercede for us, O Mother of God,
That we may find mercy in the day of judgment.
Deliver us from every evil,
And lead us to eternal joy in the kingdom of your Son,
Jesus Christ, our Lord. Amen.

47

Prayer to Our Lady, Undoer of Knots

Virgin Mary, Mother of fair love,

Mother who never refuses to come to the aid of a child in need,

Mother whose hands are filled with the healing balm of mercy—

I entrust into your loving care the knots and tangles in my life.

Please untie the knots of my sins, fears, doubts, and failures.

Bring clarity to confusion, peace to anxiety, and hope to despair.

Lead me closer to your Son, Jesus, so that through Him, All things may be made new.

O Mary, Undoer of Knots, pray for me. Amen.

Printed in Dunstable, United Kingdom